Using an FHA Cash-Out Refinance to Build Wealth

How to Turn Home Equity into Cash Without Selling Your Home

By Joseph G. Correa

Licensed Mortgage Broker, Finibi Mortgage

Copyright & Legal Notice

Published by Live Stronger Faster

First Edition, 2026

Table of Contents

Foreword

Homeownership has always been more than just a place to live. For generations, it has been one of the most reliable ways everyday people have built stability, security, and long-term wealth in the United States. Yet for many borrowers, the idea of turning homeownership into a financial tool still feels distant, complicated, or even intimidating. Too often, people are told that real estate wealth is reserved for investors, the wealthy, or those who already "made it." The truth is far simpler and far more empowering: wealth-building through homeownership is accessible to ordinary people when they understand how to use the tools already available to them. One of the most overlooked and misunderstood of those tools is the FHA cash-out refinance.

This book was written to close that gap. It exists because too many homeowners sit on growing equity without realizing what it can do for them, and too many borrowers are never taught that their home can be more than a monthly payment. Equity is not just a number on paper. When used responsibly, it can be transformed into opportunity, flexibility, and leverage. It can help eliminate high-interest debt, fund education, start businesses, improve cash flow, and create paths toward long-term financial independence. Yet equity only becomes powerful when borrowers understand how it works and how to access it safely. That is exactly what this book is designed to do.

The FHA program was created to expand access to homeownership, particularly for borrowers who may not fit traditional lending molds. Over time, it has helped millions of Americans buy homes with lower down payments, more flexible credit requirements, and more forgiving underwriting standards. What many borrowers do not realize is that FHA does not stop being useful after the purchase. FHA refinancing options, including cash-out refinances, can play a critical role in a homeowner's long-term financial strategy when used correctly. This book focuses on that next chapter of the FHA journey, the moment when a homeowner begins to ask not just how to keep their home, but how to make their home work for them.

Using an FHA cash-out refinance to build wealth is not about reckless borrowing or taking unnecessary risks. It is about intentional planning, informed decision-making, and understanding the difference between good debt and bad debt. It is about learning how to replace high-interest obligations with lower-cost financing, how to invest in assets instead of liabilities, and how to align borrowing decisions with long-term goals rather than short-term impulses. This book approaches the subject with realism and responsibility, because sustainable wealth is not built overnight and it is not built by shortcuts. It is built through strategy, patience, and education.

One of the biggest misconceptions surrounding cash-out refinancing is that it is only useful for emergencies or consumer spending. In reality, the most successful borrowers use cash-out refinances as part of a broader financial framework. They understand timing, equity growth, loan-to-value limits, and the importance of preserving long-term affordability. They know when it makes sense to pull equity and when it makes sense to leave it untouched. They treat their home as a financial foundation, not a credit card. This book was written to help readers think like those borrowers, even if they are just starting their homeownership journey.

Another reason this book matters is because misinformation is everywhere. Many homeowners receive conflicting advice from friends, online forums, social media videos, and even well-meaning professionals who do not fully understand FHA guidelines. Some are told that cash-out refinances are dangerous. Others are told they are easy money. Neither extreme is accurate. FHA cash-out refinances have specific rules, limits, benefits, and tradeoffs, and understanding those details makes all the difference. This book cuts through the noise and explains what actually matters, without jargon, hype, or fear-based messaging. Throughout the FHA Homeownership & Wealth Series, the goal has been to educate borrowers at every stage of the process, from first-time buyers to seasoned homeowners. This eighth book builds on that foundation by shifting the focus from acquisition to optimization. It recognizes that buying a home is only the beginning. What comes after the purchase often determines whether homeownership becomes a burden or a wealth-building asset. By the time readers reach this book, they are ready to think more strategically, to ask deeper questions, and to take greater ownership of their financial decisions.

This book also acknowledges that every borrower's situation is different. There is no single "right" way to use equity, and there is no universal strategy that applies to everyone. Some readers may be looking to consolidate debt and improve monthly cash flow. Others may want to fund renovations that increase property value. Some may be exploring small business opportunities, education expenses, or investment properties. The purpose of this book is not to tell readers what they must do, but to give them the knowledge they need to make informed choices aligned with their goals, risk tolerance, and life circumstances.

Responsible wealth-building requires context. It requires understanding how interest rates affect long-term costs, how mortgage insurance factors into FHA loans, how loan terms influence cash flow, and how refinancing decisions impact future flexibility. It also requires honesty about personal habits, spending patterns, and financial discipline. This book does not assume perfection. It assumes progress. It meets borrowers where they are and provides a framework for moving forward with clarity rather than confusion.

There is also an emotional component to equity and refinancing that is rarely discussed. For many homeowners, their home represents security, family, and hard-earned achievement. The idea of borrowing against it can feel uncomfortable or even frightening. That hesitation is understandable. This book respects that emotional reality while also encouraging readers to separate fear from facts. Knowledge reduces fear. Understanding replaces uncertainty with confidence. When borrowers know how FHA cash-out refinances work, what safeguards exist, and how to structure decisions responsibly, they are far better equipped to use equity as a tool rather than avoid it out of fear.

The broader mission of this series has always been empowerment. Empowerment comes from education, not sales pitches. It comes from transparency, not pressure. It comes from helping borrowers see the full picture so they can take control of their financial future. This book continues that mission by demystifying a topic that is often oversimplified or misunderstood. It gives readers the language, concepts, and practical insight they need to have informed conversations with lenders, advisors, and financial professionals.

As you read this book, you are encouraged to think long-term. Wealth is rarely built in dramatic leaps. More often, it is built through a series of smart, aligned decisions made over time. An FHA cash-out refinance is not a magic solution, but when used intentionally, it can be a powerful step in a broader journey. This book invites you to see your home not just as shelter, but as a financial asset with potential, responsibility, and opportunity.

Whether you are early in your homeownership journey or years into it, this book is designed to help you think differently about equity, leverage, and possibility. It is written for borrowers who want clarity instead of confusion, strategy instead of guesswork, and control instead of uncertainty. The pages that follow are meant to inform, guide, and empower, not to rush or persuade. The decisions will always be yours. The knowledge, however, is now within reach.

If this book helps you see your home in a new light, ask better questions, or make a more confident financial decision, then it has served its purpose. Wealth is not reserved for a select few. With the right tools and understanding, it can be built step by step, starting right where you are.

Chapter 1

The Hidden Power in Your Walls – Understanding Home Equity as a Wealth Tool

Most homeowners think of equity as something passive, a number that quietly grows over time as mortgage balances fall and property values rise. It shows up on paper statements, online dashboards, or appraisal reports, but rarely feels real or usable. For many borrowers, equity is treated as a future benefit rather than a present opportunity. Yet equity is not just a theoretical concept or a retirement footnote. It is a financial asset with real-world utility, and understanding how it works is the first step toward transforming homeownership from a fixed expense into a dynamic wealth-building tool.

Home equity represents the difference between what your home is worth and what you owe on it. That gap is not accidental. It is created through a combination of market appreciation, principal reduction, and time. Each mortgage payment slightly increases ownership. Each year of rising property values expands potential. Over time, equity accumulates quietly, often without homeowners fully realizing its scale or significance. What makes equity powerful is not simply that it exists, but that it can be accessed strategically through refinancing options such as an FHA cash-out refinance.

The idea of borrowing against your home may feel counterintuitive at first. Many people grow up hearing that debt is something to avoid, not something to use. While that mindset is rooted in caution, it often lacks nuance. Not all debt is created equal. High-interest consumer debt drains wealth, while well-structured, low-interest debt tied to appreciating assets can accelerate it. The difference lies in purpose, cost, and long-term impact. An FHA cash-out refinance allows homeowners to replace expensive debt, invest in income-producing opportunities, or reposition their finances in ways that support long-term stability rather than undermine it.

One of the most important shifts borrowers must make is moving from a consumption mindset to a strategy mindset. Equity should not be viewed as extra spending money, but as deployable capital. When homeowners see equity as capital, they begin asking different questions. How much equity do I have? What does it cost to access it? What return could I generate by using it wisely? How does this decision affect my long-term affordability and financial flexibility? These questions are foundational to responsible wealth-building and are far more important than chasing short-term gains. The FHA cash-out refinance is unique because it offers access to equity under guidelines designed to be inclusive. While conventional cash-out refinances often require higher credit scores, lower debt ratios, or stricter documentation, FHA programs were built with flexibility in mind. That flexibility does not mean recklessness. FHA still imposes loan-to-value limits, income verification requirements, and underwriting standards that protect both borrowers and lenders. Understanding those guardrails helps homeowners use the program effectively without overextending themselves.

Another overlooked aspect of equity is timing. Equity grows unevenly. Early years of a mortgage build equity slowly, while later years accelerate growth as principal reduction compounds. Market cycles also influence equity availability. Interest rates, property values, and lending guidelines all affect when and how equity can be accessed. Strategic borrowers pay attention to these cycles. They understand that the best time to refinance is not always when rates are lowest or values are highest, but when the numbers align with personal goals and long-term plans.

Equity also interacts directly with cash flow. A refinance that increases loan balance may still improve monthly affordability if it replaces higher-interest obligations. Conversely, pulling equity without improving cash flow can create financial strain even if the strategy looks sound on paper. That is why wealth-building through equity must always consider monthly impact alongside long-term benefit. Sustainability matters. Wealth that cannot be maintained eventually collapses under its own weight.

Home equity is also deeply personal. It represents years of effort, sacrifice, and commitment. For many families, it is their largest asset. Treating it casually or emotionally can lead to poor decisions, but treating it with informed respect can unlock opportunities that would otherwise remain out of reach. Education transforms equity from a vague concept into a precise instrument. When borrowers understand the math, the rules, and the implications, equity becomes something they control rather than something that controls them.

This chapter lays the foundation for everything that follows by reframing equity not as a safety net alone, but as a lever. A lever amplifies effort. Used correctly, it allows small inputs to produce large outcomes. Used incorrectly, it can cause imbalance. The goal of this book is not to push readers toward action, but to equip them with understanding so that any action they take is intentional, calculated, and aligned with their goals. Equity is neither good nor bad. It is neutral. What determines its value is how it is used.

As you move forward, keep this core principle in mind: wealth is rarely built by avoiding tools, but by learning how to use them responsibly. Your home already contains value. This book is about helping you decide whether, when, and how to put that value to work in a way that supports your future rather than compromises it.

A Numbers-Based Journey

When Maria bought her home, she did not think of it as an investment. She thought of it as stability. The purchase price was $300,000, and she used an FHA loan with a 3.5 percent down payment, putting down $10,500. Her starting loan balance was approximately $289,500. At the time, her interest rate was 5.25 percent, and her monthly mortgage payment, including mortgage insurance, came out to roughly $1,900. For Maria, the payment was manageable, and that was all that mattered.

Five years later, Maria's life looked different. Her income had increased modestly, her credit had improved, and home prices in her area had risen significantly. A recent appraisal placed her home's value at $380,000. Over five years of payments, her loan balance had dropped to approximately $270,000. Without realizing it, Maria had built about $110,000 in equity. That number surprised her. She had never thought of herself as someone with access to that kind of capital. At the same time, Maria carried $35,000 in credit card debt at an average interest rate of 19 percent. Her monthly minimum payments totaled about $900, much of which went toward interest rather than principal. She also had a small personal loan with a balance of $15,000 at 12 percent interest, costing her another $400 per month. Combined, Maria was paying $1,300 monthly on high-interest debt, limiting her ability to save or invest.

After learning about FHA cash-out refinances, Maria explored her options. FHA guidelines allowed her to refinance up to 80 percent of her home's value. Eighty percent of $380,000 was $304,000. Subtracting her existing loan balance of $270,000 meant she could potentially access around $34,000 in cash after accounting for closing costs. That amount closely matched her credit card debt.

Maria refinanced into a new FHA loan for $304,000 at a rate of 6 percent. Her new mortgage payment increased to approximately $2,050 per month, an increase of $150 compared to her previous mortgage. However, by eliminating $900 in credit card payments and $400 in personal loan payments, her total monthly obligations dropped by $1,150. Even with the higher mortgage payment, Maria improved her monthly cash flow by roughly $1,000.

Over one year, that $1,000 per month added up to $12,000. Over five years, it totaled $60,000, assuming she maintained the same spending discipline. More importantly, she replaced debt that would have taken decades to pay off with a structured mortgage that steadily reduced principal. The math changed her entire financial trajectory. What once felt like survival became progress.

Maria did not stop there. She used a portion of her improved cash flow to build an emergency fund and began contributing to a retirement account. The FHA cash-out refinance did not make her wealthy overnight, but it gave her room to breathe and a structure that supported long-term growth. By understanding the numbers and respecting the limits, Maria transformed hidden equity into tangible opportunity.

Her story illustrates a simple truth: when math meets strategy, equity becomes more than a concept. It becomes a tool.

Chapter 2

The Rules of the Game — How FHA Cash-Out Refinances Actually Work

Before home equity can be used as a wealth-building tool, borrowers must understand the rules that govern access to it. Many homeowners assume that equity automatically translates into cash, but in reality, equity is filtered through lending guidelines, risk controls, and underwriting standards. The FHA cash-out refinance is not a free-for-all. It is a structured program with specific limits designed to balance borrower flexibility with long-term affordability. Understanding these rules is not just helpful, it is essential. When borrowers know the boundaries, they can design strategies that work within them rather than being surprised by them.

At its core, an FHA cash-out refinance allows a homeowner to replace their existing mortgage with a new FHA-insured loan that is larger than the current balance, with the difference delivered to the borrower as cash. The amount of cash available depends on several interconnected factors, including the current appraised value of the property, the outstanding loan balance, FHA loan-to-value limits, mortgage insurance requirements, income qualification, and overall credit profile.

Each of these elements plays a role in determining not only how much equity can be accessed, but whether the refinance makes sense at all.

One of the most important rules borrowers must understand is the loan-to-value limit. FHA generally allows cash-out refinances up to 80 percent of the home's appraised value. This means the total new loan amount, including the cash taken out and financed closing costs, cannot exceed 80 percent of what the property is worth. This rule exists to ensure homeowners retain a meaningful equity buffer, protecting them from market fluctuations and reducing the risk of becoming overleveraged. While some borrowers view this limit as restrictive, it is actually one of the safeguards that makes FHA cash-out refinancing a more sustainable long-term option.

Occupancy is another critical requirement. FHA cash-out refinances are available only on primary residences. Borrowers must live in the home and certify their occupancy. This rule prevents speculative behavior and reinforces FHA's mission of supporting homeownership rather than investment-only strategies. For borrowers considering using equity to purchase rental properties or start businesses, this rule does not prohibit those uses, but it does require that the property being refinanced remains the borrower's primary home.

Understanding this distinction helps borrowers plan responsibly and avoid unintended compliance issues.

Income and credit still matter, even though FHA is known for flexibility. Borrowers must demonstrate the ability to repay the new loan based on verified income, acceptable debt-to-income ratios, and a history that supports responsible borrowing. While FHA allows lower credit scores than many conventional programs, cash-out refinances often receive closer scrutiny because they increase loan balances. Underwriters evaluate whether the refinance improves the borrower's financial position or introduces excessive risk. This evaluation reinforces the importance of purpose. Cash-out refinances that improve cash flow, reduce high-interest debt, or support stable income streams are generally viewed more favorably than those that simply increase spending power.

Mortgage insurance is another key component that borrowers must factor into their calculations. FHA loans require both upfront and monthly mortgage insurance premiums. While these premiums add to the overall cost of borrowing, they also enable FHA to offer more inclusive access to financing. Borrowers must evaluate whether the benefits of accessing equity outweigh the cost of mortgage insurance, particularly when refinancing from an existing FHA loan or switching from a conventional loan into FHA. The math matters, and this book emphasizes evaluating total cost rather than focusing solely on interest rates. Timing also plays a significant role in FHA cash-out refinances. Borrowers must meet seasoning requirements, including having made a minimum number of on-time payments and owning the property for a sufficient period. These rules ensure that equity used in a cash-out refinance is earned rather than artificially inflated through rapid transactions. Seasoning requirements protect both borrowers and the housing market by encouraging stability and discouraging speculative behavior.

Closing costs are another factor that must be understood clearly. Just like a purchase loan, a refinance includes appraisal fees, lender fees, title charges, and other costs. Borrowers can choose to pay these costs out of pocket or finance them into the new loan, provided the loan-to-value limit is respected. While financing costs can make sense in many scenarios, borrowers must understand how doing so affects loan balance, equity, and long-term interest expense. Transparency in these calculations prevents regret later.

One of the most common mistakes borrowers make is focusing only on how much cash they can take out rather than how the refinance reshapes their overall financial picture. A well-structured FHA cash-out refinance should align with a borrower's income, lifestyle, and long-term goals. It should feel manageable not just at closing, but years down the road. Understanding the rules allows borrowers to use the program proactively rather than reactively. This chapter is about clarity. The FHA cash-out refinance is neither complicated nor mysterious when broken down into its components. Each rule exists for a reason, and when borrowers understand those reasons, they are better equipped to design strategies that work. Wealth-building is not about bending rules. It is about mastering them. Once the rules of the game are clear, equity becomes something that can be planned around rather than guessed at.

Playing by the Rules and Winning with the Numbers

David purchased his primary residence for $260,000 using an FHA loan with a 3.5 percent down payment. His initial loan balance was approximately $251,000, and his interest rate was 4.75 percent. His monthly mortgage payment, including mortgage insurance, was about $1,650. At the time, David's income supported the payment comfortably, and his focus was simply maintaining stability for his family.

Six years later, the numbers told a different story. Comparable homes in his neighborhood were selling for around $350,000. After six years of consistent payments, David's loan balance had been reduced to approximately $230,000. His estimated equity was about $120,000, but David knew that access to that equity would be governed by FHA's loan-to-value limits. Eighty percent of $350,000 equaled $280,000. Subtracting his current loan balance meant he could potentially access about $50,000 before accounting for closing costs.

David wanted to use the funds to pay off $25,000 in student loans at 8 percent interest and $15,000 in auto loans at 7 percent interest. Combined, those loans cost him about $850 per month. After consulting with a lender, David refinanced into a new FHA loan for $280,000 at a 6.25 percent interest rate. His new mortgage payment increased to approximately $1,900 per month, an increase of $250.

However, by eliminating $850 in monthly debt payments, David reduced his total monthly obligations by $600. Over one year, that savings equaled $7,200. Over five years, assuming stable expenses, it totaled $36,000. Even after accounting for mortgage insurance and closing costs, the refinance improved his cash flow and reduced his overall financial stress.

Because David understood the FHA rules before refinancing, there were no surprises. The appraisal supported the value. The loan-to-value limit made sense. His income documentation aligned with underwriting requirements. The math worked because the strategy respected the structure of the program. By playing within the rules rather than fighting them, David turned equity into a sustainable financial advantage.

His experience shows that wealth-building is not about maximizing cash at all costs. It is about using equity intelligently, understanding constraints, and letting math guide decisions rather than emotion.

Chapter 3

Cash Flow First — Turning Equity Into Monthly Freedom, Not Monthly Stress

One of the most common mistakes homeowners make when considering a cash-out refinance is focusing on the lump sum instead of the monthly outcome. The excitement of accessing tens of thousands of dollars can easily overshadow the more important question: what does this decision do to my cash flow? Wealth is not built by one-time events. It is built by sustained, positive monthly margins that compound over time. For an FHA cash-out refinance to support wealth-building, it must improve or intentionally support cash flow, not quietly undermine it.

Cash flow is the oxygen of financial stability. Without it, even strong assets become liabilities. A home with significant equity can still create stress if the monthly payment becomes unmanageable. That is why the first rule of using equity wisely is ensuring that the refinance aligns with income reality, not income optimism. Borrowers must evaluate not only what they qualify for on paper, but what feels sustainable in real life. FHA guidelines may allow a certain payment, but personal comfort and long-term predictability matter just as much. An FHA cash-out refinance reshapes a borrower's financial structure. It consolidates obligations, extends repayment timelines, and often replaces short-term, high-interest debt with long-term, lower-interest debt. This restructuring can be incredibly powerful when done intentionally. By rolling multiple payments into one predictable mortgage payment, borrowers simplify their financial lives and often reduce monthly outflows. However, the opposite can also occur if equity is pulled without a clear purpose or if the new payment stretches the budget too tightly.

Interest rates play a crucial role in this equation. A refinance completed at a higher rate than the original mortgage can still improve cash flow if it replaces debt carrying significantly higher interest. Borrowers must learn to compare blended costs rather than fixating on the mortgage rate alone. The relevant comparison is not old mortgage versus new mortgage, but old total monthly obligations versus new total monthly obligations. When viewed through this lens, many cash-out refinances that initially seem expensive reveal themselves as stabilizing moves.

Another important factor is time horizon. Mortgage debt is amortized over decades, while most consumer debt is structured over much shorter terms. When borrowers use equity to eliminate short-term debt, they are effectively spreading repayment over a longer period. This lowers monthly payments but increases total interest paid over time. Whether this tradeoff makes sense depends on what the improved cash flow is used for. If the freed-up cash flow is consumed, the opportunity is wasted. If it is invested, saved, or used to improve financial resilience, the long-term outcome can be positive.

Cash flow should also be evaluated in context of risk. Life is unpredictable. Income can fluctuate. Expenses can rise. A refinance that leaves no margin for error creates vulnerability, even if it looks good on a spreadsheet. FHA cash-out refinances work best when they create breathing room, not pressure. Borrowers should aim for payments that allow flexibility, emergency savings, and adaptability rather than maximum leverage.

Mortgage insurance is another component that influences monthly cash flow. FHA mortgage insurance premiums increase the effective cost of borrowing and must be included in any honest cash flow analysis. While mortgage insurance enables access to equity for borrowers who might not qualify otherwise, it is still a real expense. Borrowers must account for it fully rather than treating it as an afterthought. Ignoring mortgage insurance can turn an otherwise sound strategy into a strained one.

Behavior also matters. Cash flow improvements only translate into wealth when accompanied by discipline. A refinance that eliminates credit card payments but is followed by renewed credit card spending resets the problem rather than solving it. Successful borrowers pair structural changes with behavioral changes. They treat the refinance as a reset point, not a permission slip. This alignment between structure and behavior is where equity-driven strategies either succeed or fail.

This chapter emphasizes a simple but powerful principle: equity should buy freedom, not stress. Freedom means fewer monthly obligations, more flexibility, and greater control over time and choices. Stress means higher payments, tighter margins, and constant anxiety about making ends meet. The difference is determined by math, planning, and honesty. FHA cash-out refinances can support either outcome depending on how they are used.

As you move forward in this book, keep cash flow at the center of every decision. Ask what changes monthly, not just what changes at closing. Wealth is built quietly, month by month, through choices that compound in your favor. When equity is used to improve cash flow, it becomes a stabilizing force that supports long-term growth rather than a gamble that depends on everything going right.

From Payment Pressure to Monthly Control

When Anthony refinanced his home, he was focused on solving a short-term problem. He had accumulated $42,000 in consumer debt, including credit cards, a personal loan, and medical bills. His monthly payments on that debt totaled nearly $1,100, leaving him feeling constantly behind despite earning a steady income. His home, purchased six years earlier for $275,000, had appreciated significantly, and a recent appraisal valued it at $360,000.

Anthony's existing FHA loan balance was approximately $245,000. Under FHA's 80 percent loan-to-value rule, he could refinance up to $288,000. After subtracting his current balance and estimated closing costs, he could access roughly $35,000 to $38,000 in cash. While this would not eliminate every dollar of debt, it would remove the highest-interest obligations, which carried rates between 18 and 24 percent.

Anthony refinanced into a new FHA loan for $288,000 at a 6.5 percent interest rate. His original mortgage payment had been $1,650 per month. The new payment, including mortgage insurance, increased to approximately $1,980, a rise of $330. At first glance, this increase concerned him. However, once the refinance paid off $38,000 in high-interest debt, his monthly consumer debt payments dropped from $1,100 to just $250, which included a remaining car payment. When Anthony compared his total monthly obligations before and after the refinance, the numbers told a clear story. Before refinancing, he paid $2,750 per month toward housing and debt. After refinancing, his combined obligations dropped to approximately $2,230. That difference of $520 per month represented regained control. Over a year, that amounted to more than $6,200. Over five years, it exceeded $31,000, assuming stable expenses and income.

Anthony used half of his monthly savings to build an emergency fund and the other half to accelerate principal payments on his mortgage. Instead of feeling trapped by his home, he felt supported by it. The refinance did not create wealth instantly, but it shifted his financial direction. Cash flow, not the lump sum, became the turning point.

His experience illustrates that the true value of equity is not found in how much you take out, but in how your monthly life changes afterward. When the math works in your favor, equity becomes a tool for freedom rather than a source of stress.

Chapter 4

Leverage with Purpose — When Using Equity Accelerates Wealth Instead of Delaying It

Leverage is one of the most misunderstood concepts in personal finance. For some, it represents danger and excess. For others, it is the engine behind nearly every meaningful wealth-building strategy. The difference between those two outcomes is not leverage itself, but intention. When equity is used without purpose, it can quietly delay progress and increase risk. When equity is used deliberately, aligned with clear goals and disciplined execution, it can accelerate financial growth in ways that would otherwise take decades. This chapter focuses on understanding when leverage works in your favor and when it works against you.

At its core, leverage means using borrowed capital to achieve outcomes that would be difficult or impossible using cash alone. In the context of an FHA cash-out refinance, leverage allows homeowners to access capital at relatively low interest rates compared to consumer debt or unsecured financing. This access can be transformative, but only when the cost of borrowing is justified by the outcome it enables. Borrowers must learn to evaluate not just whether they can borrow, but why they should borrow and what that borrowing is expected to produce over time.

Purpose is the filter that separates productive leverage from destructive leverage. Productive leverage tends to improve cash flow, increase income, reduce risk, or create assets that appreciate or generate returns. Destructive leverage often funds consumption, lifestyle inflation, or short-term relief without long-term benefit. An FHA cash-out refinance can support either path depending on how the proceeds are deployed. The loan itself is neutral. The results are determined by the borrower's decisions.

One of the most common productive uses of equity is investing in improvements that increase earning potential or asset value. This might include education, certifications, business formation, or home improvements that raise property value beyond their cost. Another productive use is repositioning debt in a way that improves long-term financial resilience, such as replacing variable, high-interest obligations with stable, predictable mortgage financing. These uses do not rely on speculation. They rely on math, structure, and discipline.

Risk management is inseparable from leverage. Every decision to borrow introduces obligation, and obligation must be supported by reliable income and reasonable margins. FHA cash-out refinances work best when borrowers maintain equity buffers, avoid maximum leverage, and preserve flexibility. Using all available equity may feel empowering in the moment, but it removes margin for error. Smart leverage leaves room for change. It anticipates uncertainty rather than assuming stability.

Another critical factor in evaluating leverage is opportunity cost. Equity that remains unused has a cost just as equity that is misused does. Leaving equity idle while carrying high-interest debt or missing income-generating opportunities can slow progress significantly. The question is not whether equity should ever be used, but whether its use improves the overall financial trajectory. Borrowers must compare the cost of borrowing against the cost of inaction. Often, the hidden cost of doing nothing is far greater than the visible cost of refinancing.

Leverage must also be evaluated across time. Short-term discomfort can sometimes produce long-term advantage, while short-term comfort can produce long-term stagnation. An FHA cash-out refinance that slightly increases a mortgage payment but unlocks income growth or eliminates crippling debt may feel uncomfortable initially, but beneficial over years. Conversely, using equity to fund short-lived expenses may feel painless at closing but create long-term drag. Time reveals whether leverage was purposeful or impulsive.

Behavior amplifies leverage outcomes. Borrowers who treat equity proceeds as strategic capital tend to plan, track, and adjust. They measure outcomes and make corrections when needed. Borrowers who treat equity as windfall money often drift back into old habits, recreating the very problems the refinance was meant to solve. Discipline is not optional when leverage is involved. It is the difference between progress and repetition.

This chapter emphasizes a central truth: leverage magnifies whatever already exists. If a borrower has clarity, discipline, and structure, leverage accelerates growth. If a borrower lacks those qualities, leverage accelerates problems. FHA cash-out refinances can be powerful tools for wealth-building, but only when paired with intentional planning and honest self-assessment. The goal is not to borrow more, but to borrow better.

As you continue through this book, keep asking one guiding question: does this use of equity move me closer to the life I want, or simply make the present moment easier? Wealth-building rewards patience, clarity, and alignment.

When leverage is applied with purpose, equity becomes a catalyst rather than a constraint.

Borrowing to Build Forward, Not Just Break Even

When Lena considered refinancing her home, she was not looking for relief. She was looking for acceleration. She had purchased her home eight years earlier for $240,000 using an FHA loan. Over time, property values increased steadily, and a recent appraisal valued her home at $360,000. Her remaining loan balance was approximately $215,000, giving her substantial equity.

Under FHA's 80 percent loan-to-value guideline, Lena could refinance up to $288,000. After accounting for her existing loan balance and closing costs, she had access to approximately $65,000 in cash. Rather than pulling the maximum available, Lena chose to take out $45,000, preserving additional equity as a buffer. Her new FHA loan balance became $260,000 at a 6.25 percent interest rate, increasing her monthly mortgage payment by about $275.

Lena used $30,000 of the proceeds to start a small consulting business related to her professional expertise. The remaining $15,000 was set aside as operating capital and emergency reserves. Within the first year, her business generated $2,500 per month in net income. Even after accounting for taxes and variability, the income comfortably exceeded the $275 increase in her mortgage payment. Over twelve months, Lena's additional income totaled approximately $30,000. Over three years, it exceeded $90,000. The cost of borrowing the $45,000 through her mortgage was significantly lower than alternative financing options she had considered, such as business credit cards or personal loans. By choosing leverage intentionally and conservatively, Lena transformed dormant equity into an income-producing asset.

The math reinforced her decision. Her increased mortgage payment cost roughly $3,300 per year, while her business generated more than nine times that amount annually. Even if income fluctuated, the margin remained strong. Lena did not rely on optimism. She relied on structure and numbers.

Her experience demonstrates that leverage, when paired with purpose and restraint, can accelerate wealth rather than postpone it. Equity did not solve her problems. It expanded her possibilities.

Chapter 5

The Mistakes That Steal Momentum – How Poor Equity Decisions Quietly Undermine Wealth

Most homeowners do not lose financial momentum in dramatic ways. It rarely comes from one catastrophic decision. More often, momentum is lost quietly through small missteps, misunderstood tradeoffs, and decisions made without full awareness of their long-term impact. When it comes to FHA cash-out refinances, these mistakes are especially costly because they are embedded into long-term mortgage structures. This chapter is designed to help borrowers recognize the most common equity mistakes before they make them, not through fear, but through clarity.

One of the most damaging mistakes borrowers make is using equity without a defined outcome. Pulling cash simply because it is available often leads to unfocused spending that produces no lasting benefit. Equity accessed without intention tends to disappear quickly, while the obligation remains for decades. Because mortgage debt is long-term, any use of equity should be evaluated through a long-term lens. If the benefit of the cash does not outlast the cost of borrowing it, the decision likely erodes wealth rather than builds it.

Another frequent mistake is overestimating future income. Borrowers often assume that income will rise steadily, making higher payments easier over time. While income growth is possible, it is never guaranteed. FHA cash-out refinances that rely on optimistic assumptions rather than current, stable income introduce unnecessary risk. Wealth-building strategies should be resilient to income fluctuations, not dependent on perfect conditions. Planning for stability rather than best-case scenarios creates durability.

Some borrowers focus too heavily on interest rates while ignoring total cost. While rates matter, they are only one component of the equation. Mortgage insurance, extended loan terms, financed closing costs, and the opportunity cost of equity all contribute to the true cost of a refinance. A lower rate does not automatically mean a better outcome, just as a higher rate does not automatically mean a bad one. Understanding total monthly obligations and long-term cash impact is far more important than comparing rates in isolation.

Another subtle but powerful mistake is refinancing too frequently. Each refinance resets the amortization clock, shifting payments back toward interest rather than principal.

While refinancing can be beneficial, doing it repeatedly without meaningful improvement in structure can slow equity growth and extend repayment timelines unnecessarily. FHA cash-out refinances should be strategic inflection points, not routine habits. Borrowers should be clear about what each refinance accomplishes and why it is worth resetting the loan.

Behavioral drift is another threat to equity-based strategies. Many borrowers refinance to eliminate debt, improve cash flow, or create breathing room, only to gradually return to previous spending habits. Over time, credit card balances reappear, savings shrink, and the refinance loses its intended impact. The structure changed, but the behavior did not. Sustainable wealth-building requires alignment between financial tools and personal habits. Without that alignment, even well-designed strategies fail.

There is also a tendency to underestimate the value of preserved equity. Not all equity should be used. Maintaining an equity buffer provides protection against market downturns, unexpected expenses, and future opportunities. Borrowers who extract maximum equity often feel empowered initially but find themselves constrained later. FHA's loan-to-value limits exist to prevent this outcome, but borrowers still have discretion within those limits. Using less than the maximum available often creates better long-term flexibility. Timing mistakes can also undermine momentum. Refinancing during periods of financial instability, job uncertainty, or high personal stress increases the likelihood of regret. While waiting indefinitely is not productive, acting without readiness introduces risk. Readiness means understanding the math, the rules, and the personal implications of the decision. When timing aligns with preparation, equity decisions become empowering rather than stressful.

This chapter is not about avoiding equity use altogether. It is about avoiding avoidable mistakes. FHA cash-out refinances are powerful tools, but power without understanding creates unintended consequences. By recognizing these common pitfalls, borrowers can protect their momentum and ensure that equity decisions move them forward rather than quietly holding them back.

Wealth is not just built by making good decisions. It is preserved by avoiding bad ones. Understanding what not to do is just as important as understanding what to do. As you continue through this book, view equity not as a shortcut, but as a responsibility. Used wisely, it accelerates progress. Used carelessly, it delays it in ways that are hard to see until years have passed.

The Cost of Ignoring the Second Step

When Stephanie refinanced her home, the decision felt obvious. She had purchased her home for $310,000 with an FHA loan and, after six years, the property was appraised at $405,000. Her remaining loan balance was approximately $265,000. FHA guidelines allowed her to refinance up to $324,000, giving her access to roughly $50,000 after closing costs.

Stephanie used the cash to pay off $28,000 in credit card debt and $12,000 in a personal loan. Her total monthly debt payments before refinancing were $1,050. After refinancing, her mortgage payment increased from $1,780 to $2,120, an increase of $340. However, eliminating the other debts reduced her monthly obligations by $1,050, improving her net cash flow by $710 per month.

For the first year, Stephanie felt relief. She used some of the extra cash flow to travel and upgrade her lifestyle, assuming the hard part was over. Gradually, credit card balances returned. Within two years, she had accumulated $18,000 in new credit card debt, bringing back $450 in monthly payments.

At that point, Stephanie recalculated her numbers. Her mortgage payment was still $340 higher than before the refinance, and now her total monthly obligations were only $260 lower than before instead of $710. Over two years, she had gained short-term comfort but lost long-term momentum. The refinance itself was not the mistake. The lack of a follow-up plan was.

If Stephanie had redirected even half of her $710 monthly improvement into savings or debt prevention, she could have built more than $8,500 in reserves during the first year alone. Over five years, that discipline could have exceeded $40,000. Instead, the opportunity quietly slipped away.

Stephanie's experience illustrates a critical lesson: equity creates opportunity, but only structure preserves it. Without a second step, even smart financial moves lose their power.

Chapter 6

Timing the Move — Knowing When an FHA Cash-Out Refinance Actually Makes Sense

Timing is one of the most underestimated factors in wealth-building, yet it often determines whether a good idea becomes a great decision or a costly mistake. Many homeowners focus exclusively on how much equity they have, without equal attention to when it should be accessed. An FHA cash-out refinance is not simply about eligibility or loan limits. It is about alignment. Alignment between market conditions, personal finances, and long-term goals. This chapter explores how timing transforms equity from dormant potential into strategic advantage.

One of the first timing considerations is equity maturity. Equity does not grow evenly over time. In the early years of a mortgage, payments are weighted heavily toward interest, meaning principal reduction is slow. As years pass, the pace of equity growth accelerates. Market appreciation can speed this process, but appreciation alone is not enough. Borrowers who refinance too early often discover that closing costs consume much of the benefit, leaving little meaningful gain. Waiting until equity has reached a threshold where it can materially improve cash flow or opportunity outcomes is critical.

Interest rate environments also influence timing, but not always in the way borrowers expect. Many homeowners assume that refinancing only makes sense when rates are lower than their current rate. While this is true for rate-and-term refinances, it is not always true for cash-out refinances. A higher rate can still produce a positive outcome if it replaces significantly higher-cost debt or unlocks income growth. The key is evaluating net impact rather than headline rates. Timing, in this context, is about relative cost, not absolute cost.

Life stability plays an equally important role. FHA cash-out refinances should ideally be completed during periods of income consistency and personal stability. Refinancing during job transitions, major lifestyle changes, or periods of financial uncertainty increases risk. Even if a borrower qualifies, the lack of stability can turn a reasonable payment into a stressful obligation. Timing equity use around predictability rather than ambition creates durability.

Market cycles also matter. Rising property values increase available equity, while declining markets can quickly erode it. Borrowers who wait until markets peak often find that lending guidelines tighten or appraisals fall short of expectations. Conversely, borrowers who act during periods of stable growth often find smoother approvals and more predictable outcomes. FHA cash-out refinances reward preparedness more than perfect foresight.

Seasoning requirements introduce another timing layer. FHA requires borrowers to have owned and occupied the property for a minimum period and to demonstrate a history of on-time payments. These requirements are not obstacles, but checkpoints that encourage readiness. Borrowers who plan ahead often find that by the time they meet seasoning rules, their equity position and financial clarity are stronger, making the refinance more impactful.

Another overlooked timing factor is emotional readiness. Equity decisions carry weight, and rushing them under pressure often leads to regret. Borrowers who take time to understand the numbers, the tradeoffs, and the long-term implications approach refinancing with confidence rather than anxiety. Confidence leads to better decisions and better execution.

Opportunity timing also matters. Equity is most powerful when it intersects with opportunity. That opportunity might be debt restructuring, income expansion, education, or business formation. Pulling equity without a clear destination often results in drift. Waiting until there is a defined, realistic use for the funds ensures that timing supports purpose rather than impulse.

This chapter emphasizes that the best time to use equity is not when it feels urgent, but when it feels aligned. Alignment means the numbers work, the purpose is clear, and the borrower is prepared to manage the outcome. FHA cash-out refinances reward patience and planning. They penalize haste and assumption.

Timing does not require perfection. It requires awareness. When borrowers understand where they are in their equity cycle, income cycle, and life cycle, timing becomes a strategic choice rather than a gamble. Used at the right moment, equity becomes momentum. Used at the wrong moment, it becomes friction.

Waiting One Year Changed Everything

When Carlos first considered refinancing his home, the numbers were tempting but incomplete. He had purchased his home for $280,000 using an FHA loan. Five years later, the home appraised at $350,000, and his remaining loan balance was approximately $255,000. Under FHA guidelines, he could refinance up to $280,000, leaving him access to roughly

$25,000 before closing costs. Carlos wanted to use the money to pay off $20,000 in credit card debt. His monthly payments on that debt totaled $600. Refinancing immediately would have increased his mortgage payment by about $290, while eliminating $600 in monthly debt payments, improving cash flow by $310. On paper, the refinance worked.

However, Carlos anticipated a promotion within the next year that would significantly increase his income. Instead of refinancing immediately, he chose to wait and continue paying down his mortgage and credit cards. Twelve months later, his home appraised at $375,000, and his loan balance had dropped to $245,000. This increased his accessible equity substantially.

At that point, FHA's 80 percent limit allowed a refinance up to $300,000. Subtracting his loan balance meant he could access roughly $55,000 instead of $25,000. Carlos refinanced for $295,000, using $22,000 to eliminate all remaining credit card debt and keeping the rest as reserves. His new mortgage payment increased by $320, but his eliminated debt payments totaled $600, improving his net monthly cash flow by $280.

The difference was not dramatic month to month, but the long-term math told the story. By waiting one year, Carlos doubled the equity available to him and entered the refinance with higher income, stronger reserves, and greater confidence. Over five years, his improved cash flow added up to more than $16,000. More importantly, he preserved flexibility and reduced stress.

Carlos's experience illustrates that timing is not about speed. It is about readiness. Waiting did not delay his progress. It strengthened it.

Chapter 7

The Long Game — Using FHA Cash-Out Refinances Without Sacrificing Your Future

Short-term thinking is the silent enemy of long-term wealth. Many financial decisions feel successful in the moment but quietly undermine progress years later. When it comes to FHA cash-out refinances, the difference between a strategic move and a future regret is rarely obvious at closing. It reveals itself over time. This chapter is about designing equity decisions that hold up not just this year, but ten, fifteen, and twenty years into the future.

The long game begins with understanding amortization. Mortgage payments are structured so that early payments are heavily weighted toward interest, with principal reduction accelerating later. When a borrower refinances, this clock resets. While refinancing can be beneficial, repeated resets slow equity accumulation and extend the time it takes to fully own the home. FHA cash-out refinances must therefore be evaluated not just for their immediate benefit, but for how they affect long-term ownership and net worth. One of the most important long-term considerations is opportunity cost.

Equity used today cannot be used tomorrow. Borrowers must decide whether accessing equity now creates more value than preserving it for future opportunities. This is not a question of right or wrong timing, but of alignment. Using equity to eliminate high-interest debt or invest in income-producing assets may accelerate progress. Using equity to fund short-lived consumption often delays it.

Mortgage insurance adds another long-term layer. FHA mortgage insurance premiums increase the effective cost of borrowing and may remain for the life of the loan. While this cost enables access to equity, it must be justified by the outcome it supports. Borrowers playing the long game account for mortgage insurance in their calculations rather than dismissing it as temporary or negligible.

Flexibility is another hallmark of long-term thinking. Life changes. Income fluctuates. Markets shift. Equity decisions that leave no margin for adjustment create vulnerability. FHA cash-out refinances work best when borrowers preserve buffers, maintain manageable payments, and avoid maximum leverage. The goal is not to extract the most equity possible, but to design a structure that can withstand change.

Long-term wealth-building also requires consistency. A refinance can improve cash flow, but that improvement must be directed intentionally. Monthly savings, investments, or principal reductions compound quietly over time. Without a plan for the improved cash flow, the long-term benefit dissipates. Structure creates potential. Discipline realizes it.

Another often-overlooked factor is exit strategy. Borrowers should consider how today's refinance affects future options, including selling, refinancing again, or transitioning into retirement. An FHA cash-out refinance that looks attractive today may complicate future moves if not planned with an exit in mind. Long-term thinking means considering not just where you are going next, but where you ultimately want to end up.

This chapter emphasizes patience over impulse. FHA cash-out refinances are not quick wins. They are long-term commitments. When used with foresight, they can shorten the path to financial independence. When used casually, they can extend it. The difference lies in whether the decision is anchored in long-term outcomes rather than short-term relief.

The long game rewards clarity, restraint, and follow-through. Equity is a powerful ally when treated with respect. By keeping future consequences in view, borrowers can use FHA cash-out refinances to support not just today's needs, but tomorrow's goals.

A Refinance That Still Made Sense Fifteen Years Later

When Denise refinanced her home, she was thinking beyond the next few years. She had purchased her home for $265,000 using an FHA loan and, after nine years, the property appraised at $385,000. Her remaining loan balance was approximately $235,000. FHA guidelines allowed her to refinance up to $308,000, giving her access to roughly $60,000 after closing costs.

Denise used $40,000 to eliminate a combination of high-interest debt and student loans. Her monthly payments on those debts totaled $900. Her mortgage payment before refinancing was $1,620. After refinancing into a $295,000 FHA loan at 6.25 percent, her new payment increased to $1,980, an increase of $360.

By eliminating $900 in monthly debt payments, Denise improved her net cash flow by $540 per month. Instead of increasing her lifestyle, she committed to investing $400 of that amount each month and using the remaining $140 as a buffer. Over ten years, her monthly investments totaled $48,000. With an average annual return of 6 percent, the account grew to approximately $66,000.

Fifteen years after the refinance, Denise reviewed her numbers. She had paid down a significant portion of her mortgage principal, maintained consistent investments, and preserved equity despite the refinance. The decision that once felt heavy now looked obvious in hindsight. The refinance had not delayed her future. It had supported it.

Denise's story illustrates the essence of the long game. When equity decisions are paired with discipline and foresight, their benefits compound quietly and powerfully over time.

Chapter 8

From Equity to Assets — Turning Cash-Out Proceeds Into Lasting Wealth

At some point in the FHA cash-out refinance journey, the conversation must move beyond the loan itself and toward what the loan enables. Equity is only a starting point. The true wealth-building impact comes from what equity is converted into. Cash sitting idle does not build wealth. Cash deployed intentionally into assets does. This chapter focuses on the critical transition from accessing equity to transforming it into something that continues working long after the refinance is complete.

An asset is anything that produces income, appreciates in value, or reduces future expenses in a meaningful way. When homeowners use FHA cash-out proceeds to acquire or strengthen assets, they shift from borrowing to building. This distinction matters. Borrowing alone does not create wealth. Borrowing that leads to asset creation can. The difference is subtle but powerful, and it is where many borrowers either accelerate forward or stall.

One of the most common mistakes borrowers make after receiving cash-out funds is treating the money as temporary.

Because the funds arrive as a lump sum, they often feel disconnected from the long-term mortgage obligation that created them. This psychological separation can lead to underutilization or misuse. Successful borrowers reconnect the proceeds to the purpose. They assign each dollar a role, a timeline, and an expected outcome. When cash has a job, it behaves differently.

Assets do not need to be complex or speculative. They can be practical and stable. Paying off high-interest debt is, in itself, an asset-building move because it reduces future liabilities and improves cash flow. Investing in education or skills that increase earning potential is another form of asset creation. Even home improvements that reduce maintenance costs or increase property value can qualify. The key is durability. Assets should continue producing value long after the initial use of funds.

Cash-out proceeds can also serve as bridge capital. Many wealth-building opportunities require upfront investment before producing returns. FHA cash-out refinances can provide that initial funding at a lower cost than many alternative financing options. When borrowers understand this role, equity becomes a catalyst rather than a crutch. It bridges the gap between where they are and where they want to be. Risk management remains essential during this transition. Not every opportunity justifies borrowing. Borrowers must evaluate potential assets realistically, considering cash flow stability, downside risk, and time horizon. An asset that requires constant infusion of additional cash or relies on optimistic assumptions can strain finances rather than strengthen them. FHA cash-out refinances work best when proceeds are deployed into assets that align with the borrower's experience, capacity, and tolerance for uncertainty.

Another important consideration is sequencing. Borrowers often want to pursue multiple goals simultaneously, such as investing, saving, and lifestyle improvement. While balance is healthy, spreading proceeds too thinly can dilute impact. Sequencing allows borrowers to prioritize asset creation first, then gradually expand into other goals as cash flow improves. This disciplined approach increases the likelihood that the refinance produces lasting benefits.

Tracking outcomes is another hallmark of successful asset conversion. Borrowers who measure results stay engaged. They monitor whether assets produce expected returns, reduce expenses, or improve stability. If results fall short, they adjust. This feedback loop transforms equity use from a one-time decision into an ongoing strategy. FHA cash-out refinances are not set-and-forget tools. They require stewardship. This chapter emphasizes that equity becomes wealth only when it is transformed into assets that endure. The refinance opens the door. What borrowers carry through that door determines the outcome. By focusing on asset creation rather than consumption, homeowners can ensure that the long-term value of their equity far exceeds the cost of accessing it.

Turning One Refinance Into Three Income Streams

When Marcus refinanced his home, he was determined not to waste the opportunity. He had purchased his home for $290,000 using an FHA loan. After eight years, the home appraised at $410,000. His remaining loan balance was approximately $250,000. Under FHA guidelines, he could refinance up to $328,000. After closing costs, Marcus accessed $65,000 in cash.

His mortgage payment increased from $1,720 to $2,060, an increase of $340 per month. Marcus knew that increase had to be justified by what the cash produced. He allocated the $65,000 intentionally rather than impulsively.

Marcus used $25,000 to eliminate high-interest credit card and personal loan debt that carried average interest rates of 17 percent. Those debts had cost him $780 per month. He used $20,000 as a down payment on a small rental property, structured conservatively to produce net cash flow of $350 per month after expenses. The remaining $20,000 was used to launch an online consulting service related to his professional background.

Within six months, Marcus's consulting service generated an average of $1,200 per month in net income. Combined with the $350 from the rental property and the $780 eliminated in debt payments, Marcus improved his monthly position by $2,330. After accounting for the $340 increase in his mortgage payment, his net monthly improvement was $1,990.

Over one year, that improvement totaled nearly $24,000. Over five years, assuming stable income, it exceeded $120,000. The cost of borrowing the $65,000 through his mortgage was dwarfed by the assets it created. Marcus did not rely on luck. He relied on planning, discipline, and alignment.

His experience demonstrates that equity becomes powerful when it is converted into systems that produce ongoing value. The FHA cash-out refinance was not the wealth builder. The assets were.

Chapter 9

Building Optionality — How FHA Cash-Out Refinances Create Choices, Not Obligations

True wealth is not measured only by income or net worth. It is measured by optionality. Optionality is the ability to choose. It is the freedom to change direction, say no, take advantage of opportunity, or weather uncertainty without panic. Many homeowners focus on using equity to solve immediate problems, but one of the most powerful uses of an FHA cash-out refinance is creating options that did not previously exist. This chapter explores how equity, when structured thoughtfully, expands choices rather than increasing pressure.

Optionality begins with liquidity. Equity locked inside a home is valuable, but it is not flexible. Until it is accessed, it cannot be redeployed. FHA cash-out refinances convert illiquid equity into liquid capital. That conversion alone is not wealth-building, but it creates the conditions under which wealth-building becomes possible. Liquidity provides room to maneuver. It reduces dependence on high-cost credit. It allows borrowers to act decisively rather than reactively. However, liquidity without structure can quickly become obligation.

Borrowers who extract equity without a plan often feel temporary freedom followed by long-term constraint. Payments rise, cash dissipates, and flexibility shrinks. Optionality is not created by access alone. It is created by what access enables. The goal is not to turn equity into spending power, but to turn it into resilience and choice.

One of the most valuable forms of optionality is income flexibility. When equity is used to eliminate fixed expenses or create secondary income streams, borrowers reduce reliance on any single source of income. This diversification increases stability. It allows for career changes, business exploration, or reduced work hours without financial collapse. FHA cash-out refinances can support this transition when used to fund income-producing assets or remove burdensome obligations.

Another dimension of optionality is time. Monthly cash flow improvements buy time. They reduce urgency. They allow borrowers to make thoughtful decisions rather than rushed ones. Time is often undervalued in financial planning, yet it is one of the most powerful resources equity can unlock. A refinance that improves cash flow even modestly can create space for learning, planning, and growth.

Optionality also extends to future financing. Borrowers who preserve equity and maintain strong payment histories position themselves for future opportunities, whether through additional refinancing, selling, or leveraging equity later under better conditions. Using FHA cash-out refinances conservatively keeps doors open. Overleveraging closes them.

Risk tolerance plays a role as well. Optionality increases when financial structures can absorb shocks. Medical expenses, job changes, or market downturns are inevitable over long timelines. Borrowers who use equity to build reserves or reduce volatility increase their ability to withstand these events. FHA cash-out refinances can be tools for risk reduction rather than risk amplification.

This chapter emphasizes that the highest return on equity is not always financial. Sometimes it is psychological. Knowing that you have options changes how you approach decisions. It reduces fear-driven behavior. It increases confidence. Equity, when used to create optionality, supports better decision-making across every area of life.

FHA cash-out refinances are often framed as borrowing decisions. In reality, they are design decisions. They shape the structure within which future choices are made. Borrowers who understand this treat equity with respect. They ask not only what they can do with it, but what it will allow them to do later. Optionality compounds quietly. It is rarely dramatic. It shows up when a borrower turns down an undesirable job, invests in a new skill, navigates a setback calmly, or seizes an opportunity quickly. This chapter encourages readers to view equity as a means of expanding choice rather than increasing obligation. When equity creates options, it supports a form of wealth that is both durable and deeply personal.

Buying Time Changed the Outcome

When Rachel refinanced her home, she was not chasing returns. She was chasing flexibility. She had purchased her home for $315,000 using an FHA loan. After seven years, the home appraised at $430,000. Her remaining loan balance was approximately $270,000. FHA guidelines allowed her to refinance up to $344,000, giving her access to roughly $60,000 after closing costs.

Rachel's mortgage payment increased from $1,820 to $2,150, an increase of $330 per month. Instead of spending the proceeds, she allocated them deliberately. She used $30,000 to pay off student loans and a car loan that totaled $950 per month in payments. The remaining $30,000 was placed into a high-yield savings account and conservative investment portfolio.

After the refinance, Rachel's net monthly cash flow improved by $620. That improvement did not feel dramatic, but it changed her decision-making. Within a year, her employer announced restructuring. Instead of scrambling, Rachel used her improved cash flow and reserves to take a lower-paying role with better long-term prospects. The decision reduced her income by $500 per month but did not disrupt her finances.

Over three years, Rachel's new role led to advancement and higher earnings. Had she not created optionality through her refinance, she would have remained trapped in a role she disliked out of financial necessity. The math reinforced her choice. The $330 increase in her mortgage payment bought her $950 in monthly obligation reduction and long-term flexibility.

Rachel's story illustrates that sometimes the most valuable return on equity is choice. The FHA cash-out refinance did not just restructure her debt. It restructured her options.

Chapter 10

The Wealth Blueprint — Designing a Life Where Equity Works for You

Every financial tool ultimately answers one question: what kind of life does this help you build? FHA cash-out refinances are often discussed in technical terms—loan-to-value ratios, interest rates, mortgage insurance—but their true significance lies in how they shape daily experience and long-term possibility. This final chapter brings everything together, not to promote a single strategy, but to help readers design a personal blueprint where equity serves life rather than dominates it.

A wealth blueprint is not a rigid plan. It is a framework that evolves as circumstances change. At its foundation is clarity. Clarity about income, expenses, goals, values, and tolerance for risk. Equity becomes meaningful only when placed within this context. Without clarity, even well-intentioned decisions drift. With clarity, equity becomes a flexible tool that adapts alongside life.

One of the most important elements of a sustainable wealth blueprint is balance. Balance between growth and safety, between leverage and restraint, between present enjoyment and future security. FHA cash-out refinances can support this balance when they are used to stabilize foundations first and pursue growth second. Stability creates capacity. Capacity creates opportunity.

Another essential component is sequencing. Wealth is rarely built by doing everything at once. It is built by addressing constraints in the right order. Removing high-interest debt before investing, building reserves before expanding lifestyle, improving cash flow before increasing leverage. FHA cash-out refinances are most effective when they support this sequence rather than disrupt it. When equity is used to remove bottlenecks, progress accelerates naturally.

Long-term thinking must also include identity. How borrowers see themselves influences how they use equity. Those who see themselves as passive consumers tend to use equity reactively. Those who see themselves as stewards of capital tend to use equity strategically. This shift in identity is subtle but powerful. It turns financial decisions into design choices rather than emotional reactions.

A strong wealth blueprint also anticipates change. Careers evolve. Families grow. Health fluctuates. Markets cycle. Equity decisions made today should leave room for tomorrow. FHA cash-out refinances that preserve flexibility, maintain buffers, and avoid overcommitment are better positioned to adapt. The goal is not to predict the future, but to remain resilient within it.

Another often-overlooked element is integration. Equity decisions should align with other financial systems such as retirement planning, insurance coverage, tax strategy, and estate considerations. FHA cash-out refinances do not exist in isolation. When integrated thoughtfully, they support a cohesive financial ecosystem. When isolated, they create friction.

This chapter also emphasizes reflection. Borrowers should periodically revisit their equity decisions and assess outcomes. What worked? What did not? What has changed? This reflective process transforms financial tools into learning mechanisms. It allows borrowers to refine strategies rather than repeat mistakes. Wealth-building is iterative, not static.

At its highest level, a wealth blueprint is about autonomy. Autonomy over time, choices, and direction. Equity, when used responsibly, supports autonomy by reducing dependence on high-cost debt, increasing financial buffers, and creating optionality. FHA cash-out refinances are not shortcuts. They are structural tools that, when used well, support autonomy quietly and consistently. This book does not argue that every homeowner should use an FHA cash-out refinance. It argues that every homeowner should understand it. Understanding creates choice. Choice creates power. Whether equity is used now, later, or never, informed decision-making is itself a form of wealth.

As you close this book, remember that equity is not a finish line. It is a resource earned through ownership and responsibility. When aligned with purpose, discipline, and long-term thinking, it becomes a powerful ally. The blueprint is yours to design. Equity is simply one of the tools that can help bring it to life.

One Decision, Ten Years of Compounding Clarity

When Samuel refinanced his home, he did not feel excitement. He felt resolve. He had purchased his home ten years earlier for $305,000 using an FHA loan. Over time, steady appreciation brought the home's value to $450,000. His remaining loan balance was approximately $240,000. FHA guidelines allowed him to refinance up to $360,000, giving him access to roughly $95,000 after closing costs.

Samuel resisted the temptation to use the full amount. Instead, he refinanced for $330,000, pulling out $70,000 and preserving additional equity. His mortgage payment increased from $1,680 to $2,050, an increase of $370. Samuel knew the increase had to serve a long-term plan. He used $35,000 to eliminate a combination of credit card debt and a personal loan that totaled $1,100 per month in payments. Another $20,000 was invested into professional certifications that increased his earning potential. The remaining $15,000 was placed into a reserve fund.

Within two years, Samuel's income increased by $2,000 per month as a direct result of his certifications. After accounting for the $370 increase in his mortgage payment, his net monthly improvement exceeded $2,700 when including eliminated debt payments and higher income. Over one year, that improvement totaled more than $32,000.

Samuel committed to investing $1,500 of that amount monthly. Over ten years, his total contributions reached $180,000. With an average annual return of 6 percent, the account grew to approximately $250,000. The refinance that once felt heavy became the quiet foundation of long-term growth.

Ten years later, Samuel looked back not at the loan, but at the life it supported. Reduced stress. Increased options. Financial confidence. The FHA cash-out refinance did not create wealth by itself. It enabled a blueprint that did.

His story illustrates the central lesson of this book: equity is most powerful when it is used deliberately, measured patiently, and aligned with the life you want to build.

Chapter 11

The Exit Advantage — How Smart Equity Planning Protects You on the Way Out

Most homeowners think about equity only in terms of access. How much can I pull out? What can I use it for right now? Far fewer people think about equity in terms of exit. Yet the end of a strategy is just as important as the beginning. Every FHA cash-out refinance sets conditions for future decisions, including selling the home, downsizing, upgrading, retiring, or shifting into a different phase of life. This chapter focuses on designing equity decisions that protect flexibility on the way out, not just opportunity on the way in.

An exit is not a failure. It is a transition. Homes are rarely held forever. Families grow, careers change, and priorities evolve. Equity decisions made years earlier quietly shape how smooth or stressful those transitions become. Borrowers who ignore exit considerations often find themselves trapped by high balances, limited proceeds, or timing constraints. Borrowers who plan ahead preserve optionality even as they leverage equity along the way.

One of the most important exit considerations is remaining equity at sale. Pulling equity today reduces future sale proceeds tomorrow. That tradeoff is not inherently negative, but it must be intentional. If equity is used to create assets or income that exceed the value surrendered later, the strategy succeeds. If equity is used for short-lived benefits, the exit becomes weaker. Smart borrowers evaluate equity use not just by what it produces now, but by what it leaves behind later.

Loan balance trajectory matters. FHA cash-out refinances reset amortization and increase principal balances. Over time, this affects how much equity rebuilds before a sale or next refinance. Borrowers who plan exits consider how long they expect to remain in the home and whether the equity they extract will be replaced through appreciation, principal reduction, or external investments. Time horizon turns an equity decision from a gamble into a calculation.

Another exit-related factor is market sensitivity. Borrowers who extract maximum equity leave themselves more exposed to market downturns. A modest decline in property value can dramatically affect sale outcomes when leverage is high. FHA's loan-to-value limits provide a buffer, but borrowers still control how aggressively they use available equity. Conservatism at the margin often determines whether an exit feels empowered or constrained. Cash flow also influences exit readiness. A refinance that improves monthly cash flow increases the ability to save, invest, and prepare for future transitions. Conversely, a refinance that strains cash flow reduces adaptability. Exit readiness is not just about net worth. It is about liquidity, reserves, and confidence in timing. FHA cash-out refinances that support cash flow indirectly support better exits.

Retirement planning adds another layer. Many homeowners approach retirement with significant equity but limited liquidity. Decisions made earlier determine whether that equity can be accessed comfortably or whether it remains locked behind obligations. Borrowers who align equity strategies with retirement timelines create smoother transitions. Those who ignore this alignment often face rushed or suboptimal decisions later.

Exit planning also includes emotional readiness. Financial stress at transition points amplifies uncertainty. Borrowers who preserve equity buffers and maintain flexibility approach exits calmly rather than reactively. This psychological benefit is often undervalued, yet it shapes outcomes just as powerfully as math.

This chapter emphasizes that every equity decision creates momentum in a direction. That direction may be forward, sideways, or backward depending on planning. FHA cash-out refinances can support strong exits when they are structured with awareness of future transitions. The best exits feel anticlimactic because they were anticipated rather than forced.

Wealth is not only built by entry strategies. It is secured by exits that honor the effort invested along the way. Equity, when planned with the end in mind, becomes a bridge rather than a burden.

Planning the Exit Before It Was Necessary

When Laura refinanced her home, she was not thinking about selling. She was thinking about stability. She had purchased her home for $320,000 using an FHA loan. After nine years, the property appraised at $460,000. Her remaining loan balance was approximately $255,000. FHA guidelines allowed her to refinance up to $368,000, giving her access to roughly $90,000 after closing costs.

Laura chose restraint. Instead of pulling the maximum, she refinanced for $330,000, accessing $60,000 and preserving additional equity. Her mortgage payment increased from $1,700 to $2,020, an increase of $320. She used $40,000 to eliminate high-interest debt that totaled $1,050 per month and placed the remaining $20,000 into a conservative investment account.

After refinancing, Laura's net monthly cash flow improved by

$730. She invested $500 of that amount consistently. Over seven years, her contributions totaled $42,000. With a conservative 5.5 percent average annual return, the account grew to approximately $57,000.

Seven years later, Laura received an unexpected job opportunity in another state. When she sold her home, the market value was $495,000. Her remaining loan balance was approximately $290,000. After selling costs, she walked away with more than $165,000 in equity. Combined with her investment account, she had over $220,000 available for her next move.

If Laura had pulled the maximum equity years earlier, her sale proceeds would have been dramatically lower. By planning her equity use with an exit in mind, she preserved flexibility without sacrificing opportunity. The refinance supported her life when she needed it and stepped aside when it was time to move on.

Her story illustrates a powerful truth: the best exits are designed long before they are required. Equity, when respected, rewards foresight.

Chapter 12

The Confident Borrower — Turning Knowledge Into Calm, Consistent Decisions

Confidence is often mistaken for boldness, but in financial decision-making, true confidence looks quiet. It shows up as patience, clarity, and the ability to say yes or no without anxiety. Throughout this book, the focus has been on understanding how FHA cash-out refinances work, when they make sense, and how they can support wealth-building when used responsibly. This final instructional chapter centers on the outcome of that understanding: becoming a confident borrower who makes calm, consistent decisions over time.

A confident borrower is not someone who always takes action. It is someone who understands their options well enough to choose deliberately. Knowledge transforms uncertainty into choice. When borrowers understand equity, cash flow, leverage, timing, risk, and exit strategy, they are no longer reactive. They do not refinance out of fear, urgency, or temptation. They refinance, or choose not to, based on alignment with long-term goals. One of the defining traits of a confident borrower is the ability to evaluate tradeoffs without emotion. Every equity decision involves compromise. Increased liquidity may come with higher payments. Preserved equity may come with missed opportunity. Confidence does not eliminate these tradeoffs. It allows borrowers to accept them knowingly. When decisions are made with eyes open, regret loses its power.

Consistency is another hallmark of confidence. Borrowers who understand their financial structure tend to repeat good behaviors. They save when cash flow improves. They avoid recreating debt. They revisit plans periodically and adjust as needed. FHA cash-out refinances are not one-time events in this framework. They are components of an evolving strategy that responds to life rather than fights it.

Confidence also changes how borrowers interact with professionals. Instead of deferring blindly or resisting advice reflexively, confident borrowers ask informed questions. They understand why guidelines exist. They recognize when a recommendation fits their situation and when it does not. This collaborative approach leads to better outcomes and fewer surprises.

Another important aspect of borrower confidence is restraint. Knowing you can access equity is different from believing you must. Many borrowers feel pressure to "use" available equity simply because it exists. Confidence allows borrowers to leave equity untouched when the timing or purpose is not right. This restraint often preserves flexibility and reduces stress.

Calm decision-making compounds. Over time, small, steady choices shape financial trajectories more powerfully than dramatic moves. A confident borrower may refinance once or twice over decades, each time with clear intent. They may also choose long periods of inaction when stability serves them better. Both are signs of strength, not indecision.

This chapter emphasizes that the goal of learning about FHA cash-out refinances is not to create urgency, but to create readiness. Readiness means that when circumstances align, the borrower is prepared. It also means that when circumstances do not align, the borrower is comfortable waiting. This balance is rare, and it is one of the most valuable outcomes of financial education.

As this book concludes, the central message is simple: equity is not power by itself. Understanding is power. When borrowers understand their tools, they stop fearing them and stop abusing them. FHA cash-out refinances become neither tempting nor intimidating. They become options.

The confident borrower does not chase wealth. They design stability and allow wealth to emerge over time. Equity becomes part of that design, used thoughtfully, sparingly, and purposefully. That mindset is the true asset this book aims to build.

Calm Decisions Outperformed Bold Moves

When Kevin reviewed his home equity, he felt no urgency. He had purchased his home for $300,000 using an FHA loan. After ten years, the home appraised at $465,000. His remaining loan balance was approximately $235,000. FHA guidelines allowed him to refinance up to $372,000, giving him access to more than $130,000 in potential equity.

Kevin did not rush. He reviewed his finances calmly. He had $18,000 in remaining student loan debt at 6 percent interest and a car loan balance of $14,000 at 7 percent interest. His total monthly payments on those debts were $620. His mortgage payment was $1,650.

Kevin refinanced for $280,000 instead of pulling cash. This allowed him to reduce his interest rate and monthly payment slightly while preserving equity. Two years later, after further appreciation and principal reduction, his home appraised at $500,000 and his balance had dropped to $225,000.

At that point, Kevin chose to do a modest FHA cash-out refinance to $300,000. His mortgage payment increased by

$280. He used $32,000 to eliminate his remaining debts, removing $620 in monthly payments. His net monthly improvement was $340.

Kevin invested $250 of that amount each month. Over eight years, his contributions totaled $24,000. With an average annual return of 6 percent, the account grew to approximately $36,000. More importantly, Kevin never felt rushed or stressed. Each decision followed clarity, not pressure.

By waiting and acting deliberately, Kevin preserved equity, reduced debt, and improved cash flow without overleveraging. His outcomes were not flashy, but they were durable. The math rewarded patience.

Kevin's story illustrates the final lesson of this book: confidence does not come from bold moves. It comes from understanding, timing, and the ability to act calmly when the moment is right.

Chapter 13

The Second Cycle — How to Rebuild Equity Faster After a Cash-Out Refinance

One of the most persistent myths about cash-out refinancing is that it permanently sets borrowers back. Many homeowners believe that once equity is accessed, the path forward becomes slower and more difficult. In reality, the opposite can be true when the refinance is structured correctly. A well-planned FHA cash-out refinance can shorten the time it takes to rebuild equity by improving cash flow, increasing income capacity, and creating momentum that accelerates ownership rather than delays it. This chapter focuses on what happens after the refinance, when the second equity cycle begins.

Equity rebuilding is not automatic. It is influenced by three primary forces: principal reduction, property appreciation, and behavior. Refinancing resets the loan balance, but it also reshapes monthly obligations. If the refinance improves cash flow or earning potential, it can accelerate principal reduction through extra payments or indirect investment. If it strains cash flow, equity rebuilding slows. The outcome depends less on the refinance itself and more on how the borrower responds to the new structure.

One of the most effective ways to rebuild equity quickly is by redirecting improved cash flow toward principal. Even modest additional payments can have an outsized impact over time. Mortgage amortization is front-loaded with interest, but small principal reductions early in the loan cycle reduce interest accumulation over decades. Borrowers who understand this dynamic use cash flow improvements strategically rather than passively.

Income growth plays an equally important role. FHA cash-out refinances are often used to invest in skills, businesses, or opportunities that increase earning power. When income rises faster than expenses, borrowers gain the ability to rebuild equity aggressively without sacrificing lifestyle. In this way, the refinance becomes a pivot point rather than a setback.

Appreciation also contributes to the second equity cycle, but it should never be relied upon exclusively. Markets fluctuate, and appreciation is outside the borrower's control. The most resilient equity rebuilding strategies focus on controllable factors: payments, savings, and discipline. Appreciation becomes a bonus rather than a requirement.

Behavioral alignment is critical during this phase. The period immediately following a refinance often determines long-term outcomes. Borrowers who treat the refinance as a reset moment tend to make intentional choices. They avoid recreating debt, maintain reserves, and track progress. Those who drift back into old habits often experience stagnation. The structure provides opportunity, but behavior determines whether that opportunity is realized.

Another important consideration is refinancing fatigue. Some borrowers feel tempted to refinance repeatedly as equity rebuilds. While future refinances can make sense, excessive refinancing slows equity accumulation by repeatedly resetting amortization. The second cycle should prioritize stability and compounding rather than constant optimization. Patience allows equity to rebuild naturally and predictably.

This chapter reframes the post-refinance period as an opportunity rather than a penalty. Equity rebuilding does not require sacrifice alone. It requires intention. When cash flow improves, when income grows, and when discipline is applied consistently, equity can rebuild faster than it did the first time. The second cycle often benefits from experience, clarity, and improved financial habits.

Understanding this cycle changes how borrowers approach cash-out decisions. Instead of fearing lost progress, they design for accelerated recovery. The refinance becomes a strategic pause, followed by renewed forward motion. Wealth-building is not linear. It moves in cycles. Mastering those cycles is what separates confident borrowers from reactive ones.

Rebuilding Equity Faster the Second Time

When Daniel completed his FHA cash-out refinance, he worried about starting over. He had purchased his home for $285,000 and refinanced eight years later when the home appraised at $420,000. His remaining loan balance was $240,000. He refinanced to $310,000, pulling out $55,000 to eliminate high-interest debt and fund a career transition. His mortgage payment increased by $360.

Before refinancing, Daniel's total monthly obligations were $2,850, including mortgage and debt payments. After refinancing and eliminating debt, his total dropped to $2,350, improving cash flow by $500 per month. Rather than spending the improvement, Daniel committed to a structured plan.

He applied $300 of the monthly savings toward additional principal payments on his mortgage and invested the remaining $200. Over one year, his extra principal payments totaled $3,600. Because those payments reduced the loan balance early, they lowered interest costs over the life of the loan by tens of thousands of dollars. At the same time, Daniel's career transition increased his income by $1,500 per month within two years. He maintained his original lifestyle and applied $800 of the increase toward his mortgage. Between extra payments and appreciation, his loan balance dropped to $275,000 within five years, while his home's value rose to $470,000.

Daniel had rebuilt $195,000 in equity just five years after refinancing. Before the cash-out, it had taken him eight years to build less. The difference was not luck. It was structure and behavior working together.

Daniel's story illustrates a critical lesson: the second equity cycle can move faster than the first when borrowers apply intention and discipline. A refinance does not erase progress. When designed correctly, it resets the runway for accelerated growth.

Chapter 14

Stress-Test the Strategy — Making Sure Your Equity Plan Survives Real Life

Most financial plans look good on paper. Clean numbers, stable assumptions, and predictable outcomes create a sense of control. Real life, however, is rarely that orderly. Income fluctuates, expenses rise unexpectedly, markets shift, and priorities change. The true test of any FHA cash-out refinance strategy is not how it performs in ideal conditions, but how well it holds up when reality intervenes. This chapter focuses on stress-testing equity decisions so they remain sustainable under pressure.

Stress-testing begins with humility. Borrowers must accept that uncertainty is inevitable. The goal is not to eliminate risk, but to design systems that can absorb it. FHA cash-out refinances introduce long-term obligations, and those obligations must be supported even when conditions are less favorable. A strategy that works only if everything goes right is not a strategy. It is a gamble.

One of the most important stress points to evaluate is income volatility. Even borrowers with stable employment can experience disruptions through layoffs, health issues, or industry changes. An equity strategy should assume that income may dip at some point and ensure that mortgage payments remain manageable during those periods. FHA guidelines may allow higher debt ratios, but personal stress tolerance should be stricter than underwriting minimums.

Another critical stress test involves expenses. Property taxes rise. Insurance premiums increase. Maintenance costs accumulate. Borrowers who refinance to the edge of affordability often find that these incremental increases erode comfort quickly. Equity strategies that leave room for expense growth remain resilient. Those that do not become fragile.

Liquidity is a major buffer against stress. Borrowers who use FHA cash-out proceeds to build or preserve reserves dramatically increase the survivability of their strategy. Cash reserves buy time. They reduce the need for reactive decisions and prevent minor disruptions from becoming major crises. A refinance that improves cash flow but leaves no reserves is incomplete.

Interest rate risk also deserves attention, particularly for borrowers who anticipate future refinances or moves. While FHA loans offer fixed-rate stability, future opportunities may depend on market conditions. Preserving equity and maintaining strong payment history increases flexibility regardless of rate environments. Stress-testing includes imagining less favorable refinancing conditions and ensuring the strategy still works.

Behavioral stress is often underestimated. Financial pressure affects decision-making. Strategies that require constant vigilance, aggressive discipline, or perfect execution are harder to maintain during stressful periods. Simpler strategies tend to survive longer. FHA cash-out refinances that reduce complexity, consolidate obligations, and create predictable structures are more likely to endure.

Another stress scenario involves opportunity shock. Sometimes stress comes not from loss, but from opportunity. A new job, business venture, or relocation can require capital or flexibility. Borrowers who have overleveraged equity may miss opportunities because they lack liquidity or borrowing capacity. Stress-testing includes ensuring that success does not become a constraint.

This chapter reframes caution as strength. Stress-testing is not pessimism. It is preparation. Borrowers who test their equity strategies against realistic scenarios gain confidence. They know not only that the plan works today, but that it is likely to work tomorrow under different conditions. FHA cash-out refinances can support resilient strategies when they are designed with margin, simplicity, and foresight. Stress-tested plans do not promise maximum upside. They promise survivability. Over long timelines, survivability is what allows compounding to do its work.

When the Numbers Were Tested

When Olivia refinanced her home, the math worked comfortably. She had purchased her home for $295,000 and refinanced nine years later when the property appraised at $440,000. Her remaining loan balance was $250,000. She refinanced to $315,000, pulling out $55,000 to eliminate debt and build reserves. Her mortgage payment increased by $350.

Before refinancing, Olivia's total monthly obligations were $2,900. After refinancing and eliminating debt, they dropped to $2,450, improving cash flow by $450 per month. She saved $300 of that amount and used the rest to improve quality of life.

Two years later, Olivia faced an unexpected challenge. Her employer reduced hours temporarily, cutting her income by $1,200 per month. Because she had built reserves using refinance proceeds and ongoing savings, she was able to cover the gap without stress. Her mortgage payment remained manageable, and her strategy held. Over six months, Olivia used $4,800 from reserves while her income stabilized. When her hours returned, she replenished the savings gradually. The refinance did not create the challenge, but it provided the structure that allowed her to navigate it calmly.

Five years after refinancing, Olivia reviewed her progress. Her loan balance had dropped to $285,000, her home value had increased to $480,000, and her reserves exceeded $25,000. The strategy survived real life because it had been designed for it.

Olivia's story highlights the final lesson of this chapter: the best equity strategies are not the most aggressive ones. They are the ones that still work when conditions change. Stress-testing turns good math into durable wealth.

Chapter 15

The Legacy Effect — Using Home Equity to Shape the Life You Leave Behind

At the highest level, wealth is not about accumulation alone. It is about impact. The decisions borrowers make with their home equity do not end when a loan is paid off or a property is sold. Those decisions ripple outward, shaping opportunities, stability, and mindset for years to come. This chapter explores how FHA cash-out refinances, when used intentionally, can support not just personal wealth, but a broader legacy rooted in security, education, and choice.

Legacy does not require extraordinary wealth. It requires consistency, foresight, and alignment. For many families, the home is the single largest asset they will ever own. How that asset is managed determines whether it becomes a burden, a safety net, or a platform for generational stability. Equity decisions made today quietly influence tomorrow's options for spouses, children, and dependents.

One of the most powerful legacy outcomes equity can support is financial stability during transitions. Education costs, caregiving responsibilities, relocations, and career pivots often arrive without perfect timing. Borrowers who use equity to reduce volatility and increase flexibility create smoother transitions not only for themselves, but for those who depend on them. FHA cash-out refinances can support this role when they are used to strengthen the household rather than strain it.

Another legacy dimension is modeling behavior. Children and family members absorb financial habits through observation. A home that is managed thoughtfully, with equity used responsibly, teaches discipline, planning, and restraint. Conversely, repeated financial stress teaches fear and avoidance. Equity strategies that prioritize calm decision-making leave behind more than assets. They leave behind perspective.

Education is another area where equity can produce long-term legacy impact. Whether funding formal education, professional training, or entrepreneurial learning, investments in human capital often outlast financial assets. FHA cash-out refinances can make these investments accessible without resorting to high-interest debt. When education increases earning capacity or resilience, its return compounds across decades.

Legacy planning also requires thinking beyond ownership. What happens if the home is sold? What happens if it is passed on? What happens if circumstances change unexpectedly?

Equity decisions that preserve buffers and reduce leverage make all of these scenarios easier to navigate. FHA cash-out refinances that leave room for flexibility protect future choices rather than locking them in.

Another overlooked aspect of legacy is dignity. Financial stress erodes dignity over time. Constant anxiety about payments, debt, or instability affects health, relationships, and confidence. Equity strategies that reduce stress contribute to a quality of life that is felt daily. That lived experience is part of the legacy left behind.

This chapter emphasizes that legacy is not created in a single decision. It is created through patterns. Using equity sparingly. Investing in stability. Avoiding unnecessary risk. Revisiting plans periodically. FHA cash-out refinances can support these patterns when they are approached as tools rather than shortcuts.

The legacy effect also includes what is not done. Choosing not to extract maximum equity. Choosing not to refinance impulsively. Choosing not to chase short-term comfort at the expense of long-term security. These quiet decisions often matter more than dramatic ones.

As this book concludes its instructional arc, the message is clear: equity is a responsibility as much as it is an opportunity.

When used thoughtfully, it supports lives that feel stable, flexible, and intentional. That stability becomes the foundation upon which future generations stand.

The true measure of a successful equity strategy is not how much was borrowed, but how life felt afterward. Calm. Capable. Prepared. That is legacy.

A Decision That Echoed Forward

When Michael refinanced his home, he was thinking about his family, not returns. He had purchased his home for $330,000 using an FHA loan. After twelve years, the property appraised at $510,000. His remaining loan balance was approximately $245,000. FHA guidelines allowed him to refinance up to $408,000, giving him access to more than $150,000 in potential equity.

Michael chose restraint. He refinanced for $320,000, pulling out $75,000 and preserving significant equity. His mortgage payment increased by $390. He used $40,000 to eliminate lingering debt that totaled $1,200 per month. Another $25,000 was set aside in a 529 education savings plan for his children. The remaining $10,000 became an emergency fund.

After refinancing, Michael's net monthly cash flow improved by $810. He invested $500 of that amount monthly. Over ten years, his contributions totaled $60,000. With an average annual return of 6 percent, the account grew to approximately $83,000.

When Michael's eldest child entered college, tuition was covered without stress. When an unexpected medical expense arose, the emergency fund absorbed it. When Michael later sold the home, appreciation and preserved equity allowed him to transition smoothly into a new phase of life.

If Michael had extracted maximum equity, the outcome would have been very different. By prioritizing stability and foresight, he turned one refinance into a decade of calm decisions. The math supported the mindset.

Michael's story illustrates the deepest lesson of this book: wealth is not what you accumulate. It is what your decisions make possible for the people who follow you.

Final Thoughts

Homeownership is often described as a milestone, but in reality, it is a platform. What happens after the purchase matters just as much as the purchase itself. Throughout this book, the goal has not been to convince you to use an FHA cash-out refinance, but to help you understand it deeply enough to decide with confidence. Knowledge creates freedom. When borrowers understand how equity works, how it grows, how it can be accessed, and how it can be preserved, they move from passive ownership to intentional stewardship.

Equity is not luck. It is earned. It represents years of payments, patience, and responsibility. Because of that, it deserves respect. Treating equity casually leads to regret. Treating it fearfully leads to stagnation. Treating it thoughtfully leads to alignment. The difference lies in understanding. This book exists to replace uncertainty with clarity so that equity decisions become calm choices rather than emotional reactions.

One of the most important ideas woven throughout these chapters is that wealth-building is not about single moments. It is about systems. A refinance is a moment. Cash flow is a system. A lump sum is a moment. Discipline is a system. FHA cash-out refinances are powerful only when they are integrated into systems that support long-term stability, flexibility, and growth. Without that integration, even good decisions lose their impact over time.

Another central theme is restraint. Having access to equity does not mean it must be used. Some of the strongest financial positions are built by borrowers who know they could act, but choose not to until the timing and purpose align. This restraint is not hesitation. It is maturity. It reflects confidence rather than fear. It preserves options and reduces pressure.

This book has also emphasized realism. Life is unpredictable. Income changes. Markets shift. Expenses rise. The strongest equity strategies are not the most aggressive ones, but the most resilient ones. Plans that survive real life outperform plans that rely on perfect conditions. FHA cash-out refinances that leave margin, preserve buffers, and improve cash flow are far more likely to support long-term success than those that chase maximum leverage.

There is also a human side to every equity decision. Numbers matter, but so does peace of mind. Financial stress compounds quietly and affects health, relationships, and confidence. Conversely, financial stability creates space. Space to think clearly. Space to plan. Space to respond rather than react.

Many of the most valuable outcomes of responsible equity use are not visible on a balance sheet, but they are felt daily.

As you reflect on what you have learned, remember that understanding is the real asset. Whether you choose to use an FHA cash-out refinance now, later, or never, you are no longer guessing. You know the rules. You understand the tradeoffs. You can ask better questions and evaluate advice more critically. That alone changes outcomes.

Wealth is not built by avoiding tools. It is built by mastering them. FHA loans were designed to expand access to homeownership, but their value does not end at closing. When used responsibly, they can support stability, opportunity, and long-term planning. When misunderstood, they can create confusion and regret. Education is what separates those paths.

The most important takeaway from this book is not a formula or a strategy. It is a mindset. A mindset that sees equity as a resource, not a temptation. A mindset that values calm over urgency, structure over impulse, and long-term alignment over short-term relief. That mindset will serve you well far beyond this book.

As you move forward, revisit your goals periodically. Reassess your numbers. Adjust as life evolves. Financial confidence is not a destination. It is a practice. Each thoughtful decision reinforces it. Each avoided mistake preserves it. Over time, those choices compound quietly into stability and opportunity.

If this book has helped you see your home differently, ask better questions, or feel more grounded in your financial decisions, then it has done its job. Equity is not the end of the story. It is one of the tools that can help you write it intentionally.

The FHA Homeownership & Wealth Series

Complete Roadmap: From First-Time Buyer to Long-Term Wealth Builder

The FHA Homeownership & Wealth Series is designed as a progressive journey. Each book builds on the previous one, guiding borrowers from basic understanding to confident ownership, strategic financing, and long-term wealth creation. Readers can enter at any stage, but those who follow the full roadmap gain the clearest, fastest path to results.

This series is structured to meet borrowers exactly where they are—and show them what comes next.

Phase 1: Foundation & Confidence (Books 1–3)

Understanding FHA and realizing you qualify

These books eliminate confusion, fear, and misinformation. They are designed to answer the most important early question: *Is homeownership actually possible for me?*

Book 1 – FHA Loans Explained for Beginners How FHA Mortgages Work, Who Qualifies, and Why They're One of the Easiest Paths to Homeownership This is the foundation of the entire series. Readers learn how FHA loans work, why they exist, and how to evaluate FHA realistically using math instead of myths. This book builds confidence and replaces hesitation with clarity.

Book 2 – Buying Your First Home with FHA A Step-by-Step Guide to Purchasing a Home with Low Down Payment and Flexible Credit Rules This book turns understanding into action. Readers learn the full buying process—from pre-approval to closing—so they know exactly what to expect and how to avoid common first-time buyer mistakes.

Book 3 – FHA Loans for Borrowers with Low Credit or Past Credit Issues How to Get Approved with FHA Even with Late Payments, Collections, or a Low Credit Score This book is for borrowers who believe their credit disqualifies them. It explains FHA's second-chance philosophy and shows how recovery, not perfection, determines approval.

Phase 2: Income Reality & Property Flexibility (Books 4–6)

Qualifying with real-life finances and real homes

These books expand what readers believe is possible by addressing income types, property types, and cash requirements.

Book 4 – FHA Loans for Self-Employed, 1099 & Gig Workers How Business Owners and Independent

Contractors Qualify for FHA Home Loans This book demystifies income calculations for non-traditional earners and shows how FHA accommodates modern work patterns.

Book 5 – FHA Loans for Fixer-Uppers, Condos & Non-Perfect Homes How to Buy Homes That Need Repairs or Don't Fit Traditional Loan Guidelines Readers learn how FHA views property condition and how renovation and condo options expand buying opportunities.

Book 6 – FHA Loan Limits, Down Payment & Closing Costs How Much You Can Borrow and How to Bring Less Money to the Closing Table This book focuses on numbers. Readers learn how FHA loan limits work, how to reduce cash to close, and how seller credits and assistance programs change affordability.

Phase 3: Optimization & Refinancing Strategy (Books 7–8)

Using FHA beyond the purchase

These books show how FHA loans evolve with the borrower.

Book 7 – FHA Refinance Options Made Simple Streamline, Rate-and-Term, and Cash-Out Refinancing Explained for Homeowners Readers learn how FHA supports refinancing, payment reduction, and financial repositioning over time.

Book 8 – Using an FHA Cash-Out Refinance to Build Wealth How to Turn Home Equity into Cash Without Selling Your Home This book introduces equity as a strategic tool, not just a number on paper, while emphasizing responsible use.

Phase 4: Income & Expansion (Books 9–10)

Turning ownership into leverage

These books shift the reader from homeowner to strategist.

Book 9 – Buying Multi-Unit Homes with FHA How to Purchase 2–4 Unit Properties, Live in One, and Rent the Rest Readers learn how FHA enables owner-occupied investing and rent-offset strategies that dramatically reduce housing costs.

Book 10 – FHA Loan Myths, Mistakes & Borrower Strategies What Most Buyers Get Wrong—and How Smart Borrowers Win with FHA Loans This is the strategic wrap-up book that reinforces best practices, avoids costly errors, and helps readers think like informed borrowers.

About the Author

Joe Correa is a mortgage professional, educator, and financial strategist dedicated to helping everyday people understand homeownership, credit, and wealth-building without confusion or intimidation. With years of hands-on experience in the mortgage industry, Joe has worked with first-time buyers, self-employed borrowers, credit-challenged families, and aspiring investors who were often told "no" before learning what was actually possible.

What sets Joe apart is his ability to translate complex lending rules into clear, practical guidance. Rather than relying on theory, his work is grounded in real-world scenarios, real numbers, and real borrower outcomes. He believes that most people do not fail to buy homes because they lack income or discipline, but because they lack accurate information. His mission is to replace myths with math and fear with understanding.

Joe specializes in FHA loans because he has seen firsthand how transformative they can be when used correctly. He views FHA not as a last resort, but as one of the most powerful entry points into homeownership and long-term wealth—especially for borrowers navigating modern financial realities such as student loans, variable income, credit recovery, or limited savings. Through his writing, Joe teaches borrowers how to think strategically, act confidently, and use lending tools intentionally rather than emotionally.

In addition to his mortgage work, Joe is the creator of multiple educational programs and book series focused on homeownership, credit building, refinancing strategies, and financial independence. His approach emphasizes sustainability over speculation and progress over perfection. He is known for breaking down decisions into simple frameworks that empower readers to make smart choices at every stage of their journey.

Joe's writing style reflects his core belief: financial education should be accessible, practical, and empowering. He does not promise shortcuts or hype outcomes. Instead, he provides clarity, structure, and realistic paths forward—so readers can move from uncertainty to ownership with confidence.

When he is not writing or working with borrowers, Joe continues developing educational resources designed to help families build stability, equity, and long-term opportunity through informed financial decisions.

How to Get a Personalized FHA Review

If you found this book helpful, you may want to see how FHA loan options apply to your specific income, credit profile, cash to close, and homeownership goals.

Every borrower's situation is different. FHA guidelines, loan limits, interest rates, mortgage insurance, and available options vary based on income type, credit history, debt levels, savings, property type, and state guidelines. The examples in this book are educational, but your personal FHA eligibility, payment range, and strategy can only be determined through an individualized review.

As a licensed mortgage broker, I offer a **Personalized FHA Review** designed to show you: • Whether you currently qualify for an FHA loan • Your realistic home price and monthly payment range • How much cash you may need for down payment and closing costs • How credit, debt, or income factors affect your approval • Whether FHA is the best option for you now or later • What steps, if any, would strengthen your position

This review is fast, confidential, and focused entirely on helping you make informed homeownership decisions—without pressure or obligation.

To request your personalized FHA review, visit:https://finibimortgage.carrd.co/

You may also submit your information through the QR code provided in this book.

Your financial profile already tells a story.This review shows you how FHA lenders will read it.

Yours truly,

Joseph G. Correa

Licensed Mortgage Broker, Finibi Mortgage

Educational & Financial Disclaimer

This book is provided for educational and informational purposes only. The content is intended to help readers better understand FHA loans, homeownership concepts, and general mortgage strategies, but it does not constitute financial advice, legal advice, tax advice, or lending approval. Mortgage guidelines, FHA requirements, interest rates, loan programs, and qualification standards are subject to change and may vary based on individual circumstances, lender overlays, geographic location, and market conditions.

Nothing in this book should be interpreted as a guarantee of loan approval, loan terms, interest rates, or eligibility. All examples, scenarios, calculations, and illustrations are for educational purposes only and are not intended to represent actual loan offers or outcomes. Individual results will vary based on credit profile, income stability, debt obligations, assets, property characteristics, and lender-specific requirements.

Readers are encouraged to consult with a licensed mortgage professional, financial advisor, tax professional, or legal advisor before making any financial or real estate decisions. This book does not replace personalized advice or professional review. Any decisions made based on the information in this book are the sole responsibility of the reader.

The author and publisher are not responsible for any actions taken by readers as a result of the information provided in this book. While every effort has been made to ensure accuracy at the time of publication, no representation or warranty is made regarding the completeness, reliability, or current applicability of the information contained herein.

By reading this book, you acknowledge that homeownership and mortgage decisions involve risk and personal responsibility, and you agree that the author and publisher are not liable for any financial outcomes, losses, or damages that may result from reliance on this material.

This book is designed to educate, not to instruct or advise on individual financial decisions. Its purpose is to provide general understanding so readers can ask better questions, seek appropriate professional guidance, and make informed choices based on their unique circumstances.

Risk Disclosure

Homeownership and mortgage financing involve financial risk. While FHA loans are designed to increase access to homeownership and provide flexible qualification standards, they do not eliminate risk, and outcomes may vary based on individual circumstances, market conditions, and personal financial decisions. Purchasing or refinancing a home requires a long-term financial commitment and should be evaluated carefully.

Housing markets can fluctuate. Property values may increase or decrease over time, and there is no guarantee that a home will appreciate in value. Economic conditions, interest rate changes, local market factors, and unforeseen events can affect property values, mortgage payments, and resale opportunities. Borrowers should be prepared for the possibility that home values may remain flat or decline during certain periods.

Mortgage payments represent a fixed obligation that must be met regardless of changes in income, employment status, health, or personal circumstances. Failure to make mortgage payments may result in late fees, credit damage, default, or foreclosure. Borrowers should ensure they have adequate income stability, savings, and contingency planning before entering into any mortgage obligation. FHA loans include mortgage insurance, which increases the total cost of borrowing. While mortgage insurance enables access to lower down payments and more flexible credit standards, it may remain in place for a significant portion of the loan term unless refinanced or otherwise removed under applicable guidelines. Borrowers should understand how mortgage insurance affects monthly payments and long-term costs.

Refinancing, selling, or leveraging home equity is not guaranteed to be available in the future. These options depend on market conditions, interest rates, credit profile, equity levels, and lender requirements at the time of action. Borrowers should not assume future refinancing opportunities or equity access when making initial homeownership decisions.

Rental income, including income from multi-unit properties or converted rentals, is not guaranteed. Vacancies, maintenance costs, market conditions, tenant behavior, and regulatory changes can impact rental cash flow. Borrowers considering rental strategies should evaluate these risks carefully and avoid relying on projected rental income for financial stability.

This book does not provide investment advice or predict financial outcomes. All examples and scenarios are illustrative only and should not be relied upon as forecasts or guarantees.

Readers are responsible for conducting their own due diligence and seeking professional advice when appropriate.

By choosing to pursue homeownership or mortgage financing, readers acknowledge the presence of risk and accept responsibility for their financial decisions. The author and publisher are not responsible for any losses, damages, or adverse outcomes resulting from actions taken based on the information provided in this book.

This disclosure is intended to promote informed decision-making, not discourage homeownership. Understanding risk is a critical part of using FHA loans responsibly and sustainably.

www.ingramcontent.com/pod-product-compliance
Ingram Content Group UK Ltd.
Pitfield, Milton Keynes, MK11 3LW, UK
UKHW020158290926
15471UKWH00005B/938

9 798295 619403